AF270417

# BOSTON RED SOX

BY DAVID J. CLARKE

SportsZone

An Imprint of Abdo Publishing
abdobooks.com

abdobooks.com

Published by Abdo Publishing, a division of ABDO, PO Box 398166, Minneapolis, Minnesota 55439. Copyright © 2023 by Abdo Consulting Group, Inc. International copyrights reserved in all countries. No part of this book may be reproduced in any form without written permission from the publisher. SportsZone™ is a trademark and logo of Abdo Publishing.

Printed in China.
102022
012023

Cover Image: G. Fiume/Getty Images Sport/Getty Images
Interior Photos: Billie Weiss/Boston Red Sox/Getty Images Sport/Getty Images, 4, 40; Sean M. Haffey/Getty Images Sport/Getty Images, 7; Mark Rucker/Transcendental Graphics/Getty Images Sport/Getty Images, 9, 14; FPG/Archive Photos/Getty Images, 11; George Rinhart/Corbis Historical/Getty Images, 12; Bettmann/Getty Images, 16; Focus on Sport/Getty Images, 19, 27; Tony Tomsic/AP Images, 20; Focus on Sport/Getty Images Sport/Getty Images, 23; Rich Pilling/MLB Photos/Getty Images Sport/Getty Images, 24; Harry Cabluck/AP Images, 26; Rusty Kennedy/AP Images, 28; Ezra Shaw/Getty Images Sport/Getty Images, 30; Al Bello/Getty Images Sport/Getty Images, 33; Brad Mangin/MLB Photos/Getty Images Sport/Getty Images, 35; Rich Pilling/MLB/Getty Images, 37; Elsa/Getty Images Sport/Getty Images, 38; Adam Glanzman/MLB/Getty Images, 41

Editor: Steph Giedd
Series Designer: Becky Daum

**Library of Congress Control Number: 2022940391**

**Publisher's Cataloging-in-Publication Data**

Names: Clarke, David J., author.
Title: Boston Red Sox / by David J. Clarke
Description: Minneapolis, Minnesota: Abdo Publishing, 2023 | Series: Inside MLB | Includes online resources and index.
Identifiers: ISBN 9781098290115 (lib. bdg.) | ISBN 9781098275310 (ebook)
Subjects: LCSH: Boston Red Sox (Baseball team)--Juvenile literature. | Baseball teams--Juvenile literature. | Professional sports--Juvenile literature. | Sports franchises--Juvenile literature. | Major League Baseball (Organization)--Juvenile literature.
Classification: DDC 796.35764--dc23

# CONTENTS

# CHAPTER 1

# BOSTON'S BEST

As the Boston Red Sox came to bat in the top of the ninth inning in Game 4 of the 2018 World Series, baseball fans everywhere had to wonder what was in store. The Red Sox and Los Angeles Dodgers were tied 4–4. Less than 24 hours earlier, the teams had played an epic Game 3. The contest lasted 18 innings and took 7 hours and 20 minutes to complete. Finally, the Dodgers walked off a 3–2 victory to end the longest World Series game ever. The result trimmed Boston's lead in the series to 2–1.

Now Game 4 was looking like it could be headed for extra innings too. With one out, Boston second baseman Brock Holt did his best to stop that. He chopped a bouncing ball

Red Sox second baseman Brock Holt celebrates after his ninth-inning double against the Los Angeles Dodgers in Game 4 of the 2018 World Series.

just inside third base and down the left-field line. By the time the ball was quickly thrown back into the infield, Holt was on second base.

That brought up pinch hitter Rafael Devers. The 22-year-old had started the first three games of the World Series at third base but struggled. He was just 1-for-9 with five strikeouts. Now he dug in against Dodgers' reliever Dylan Floro. On the knob of Devers's bat read a message that said, "Do damage."

After watching the first two pitches miss the strike zone, Devers did his damage on the 2–0 offering. He slashed a grounder up the middle and into center field. Holt scrambled home from second base, and just like that, Boston led 5–4. The visiting Red Sox fans who had traveled from all over the country to Los Angeles's Dodger Stadium let out a thunderous cheer. Two innings earlier, Boston had trailed 4–0. Now a victory was in sight. And beyond that, Boston's fourth championship of the 2000s was within reach.

## AMERICAN ORIGINALS

The Boston Red Sox have been around since the start of the 1900s. And for nearly 100 years, the team was associated with failure. From 1919 to 2003, the supposedly "cursed" Red Sox specialized in getting close to the championship but ultimately breaking their loyal fans' hearts. However, in the Red Sox's

Boston pinch hitter Rafael Devers, *right*, celebrates after driving in the go-ahead run in Game 4 of the 2018 World Series.

early years, the team did just the opposite. The Red Sox were a powerhouse from the start.

In 1901 baseball had only one "major" league—the National League (NL). But several owners of the Western League wanted to change that. Led by its president, Ban Johnson, the Western League changed its name to the American League (AL) in 1900. A year later, the AL declared itself a major league and began to challenge the NL for the game's best players.

The AL originally did not have a team in Boston. But the NL had a Boston team, known among other teams as the Braves, from 1876 to 1952. The AL franchise that eventually became the

Red Sox was supposed to play in Buffalo, New York. However, at the last minute, Johnson decided to pull the Buffalo team out and move it to Boston.

The team, which was originally named the Americans, found a home at the quirky Huntington Avenue Grounds. The stadium fence was more than 500 feet (152 m) from home plate in center field. It also had a tool shed in the field of play. And the outfield featured several sand patches where the grass would not grow. Nearly 300,000 fans came through the gates to see Boston win 79 games in its first year. Two seasons later, the Americans finished first in the AL.

## WORLD SERIES CHAMPS

Boston jumped to 91 wins in 1903, by far the best in the AL. That season also brought a new concept to baseball. The NL champion Pittsburgh Pirates agreed to play the Americans in a postseason series. On October 1, 1903, the first World Series game was played at the Huntington Avenue Grounds. Pittsburgh won 7–3 on its way to a 3–1 lead in the series. But led by star pitchers Cy Young and Bill Dinneen, Boston charged back. Each pitcher won twice as the Americans took the next four games to win the best-of-nine series 5–3.

A year later, Boston won 95 games. But this time the race in the AL was much closer. On the final day of the season, Boston

traveled to New York for
a doubleheader with the
New York Highlanders.
Boston needed to
win only one game to
clinch the pennant. The
Americans did it in the
opener, rallying from 2–0
down to win 3–2 with a
run in the top of the ninth
inning. It was the first
showdown in what would
become one of baseball's
most heated rivalries.
Less than a decade later,
the Highlanders would
change their name to the Yankees.

Boston ace Cy Young still holds numerous career pitching records. An award named after him is now given to the best pitcher in each league after every season.

## DYNASTY YEARS

At the time, there were no playoffs, so the best team in each league advanced right to the World Series. Despite winning the AL in 1904, Boston did not get to play in the World Series again. The NL-champion New York Giants refused to play, considering the AL to be inferior. It took another eight years for Boston to get back. By 1912 a new crop of talented players had emerged for the team now known officially as the Red Sox.

The team featured what was known as the "Golden Outfield." Left fielder Duffy Lewis had a team-high 109 runs batted in (RBIs). Right fielder Harry Hooper had great speed and was one of the better defenders in the league. But center fielder Tris Speaker was the Red Sox's best player. His Most Valuable Player (MVP) season, along with 34 wins from right-handed pitcher "Smoky" Joe Wood, helped Boston back to first place.

By now the World Series was established as an annual event. This time the Giants could not back out. And the two teams played one of the most exciting World Series yet. After the second game was declared a 6–6 tie due to darkness, the series went to a decisive eighth game. Game 8 was tied 1–1 heading into the 10th inning, but the Giants scored a run off of Wood in the top of the inning to go ahead. Pinch hitter Clyde Engle

## FENWAY PARK

Boston center fielder Tris Speaker led the league in doubles in two of his seasons with the Red Sox.

led off the bottom of the inning for Boston. He hit a lazy fly ball. Giants center fielder Fred Snodgrass nearly got the out, but he dropped the ball. That started a two-run Boston rally that ended when third baseman Larry Gardner hit a sacrifice fly to bring home second baseman Steve Yerkes for the game-winning run. It was the first time the World Series had ever ended on a walk-off play. And it was the start of a dynasty in Boston.

# THE CURSE OF THE BAMBINO

After winning the 1912 World Series, Boston needed three years to get back. In 1915 the Red Sox won 101 games. After falling behind 1–0 in the World Series to the Philadelphia Phillies, the Red Sox won four straight one-run games. Harry Hooper clinched Game 5 with a home run in the top of the ninth inning to break a 4–4 tie. But the real stars of the series were Boston's pitchers. Rube Foster, Ernie Shore, and Dutch Leonard pitched every inning of the series. They allowed only nine earned runs.

The trio was so good Boston didn't need any help from Smoky Joe Wood. They also didn't need the other starter, a stocky 20-year-old named George Herman "Babe" Ruth.

Slugger Babe Ruth led the AL in home runs, runs, and RBIs in 1919, his last season with the Red Sox.

Ruth could do everything on a baseball field. In 1915 he won 18 games as a pitcher. In an era when home runs were rare, Ruth led the Red Sox with four.

In 1916 Boston repeated as champions. This time Ruth played a crucial role in the World Series. He played only one game, but it was a memorable 14-inning, 2–1 Red Sox victory in Game 2. Ruth pitched all 14 innings against the Brooklyn Robins.

Ruth's legend was only growing. He tied for the team lead in homers again in 1916, even though he only batted in 68 games. When the Red Sox made it back to the World Series two years later, Ruth was baseball's main attraction. He hit 11 home runs in 1918. That was more than four AL teams. He also went 13–7 on the mound.

Ruth played for the Red Sox from 1914 to 1919 before being traded to the New York Yankees.

Ruth batted only five times in the World Series. But he won two pitching starts as the Red Sox won again, this time 4–2 over the Chicago Cubs.

## THE SALE

The Red Sox won the 1918 World Series under the ownership of theater producer Harry Frazee. He had bought the team for $675,000 just after the 1916 World Series win.

Almost as soon as he bought the team, Frazee began struggling with money. The Red Sox were still making payments for Fenway Park. And Frazee's Broadway shows were not successful at the time. His only solution was to start selling his players. The biggest move came on December 26, 1919.

Ruth had started playing more in the outfield during the 1919 season. He set a Major League Baseball (MLB) record with 29 home runs. But he didn't get along with Frazee, and the team needed more funds. So Frazee decided to get rid of his star. He sold Ruth's contract to the New York Yankees for $100,000. Boston fans never forgave the owner.

It was easy to see why. The move flipped the AL around. The Yankees had never won a pennant before Ruth arrived. They went on to become a dynasty. The Red Sox went in the opposite direction. It would be nearly 90 years before Boston celebrated another championship. The switch in fortunes became known as "the Curse of the Bambino," after one of Ruth's nicknames.

## THE SPLENDID SPLINTER

Without Ruth, Boston struggled. From 1920 to 1933, the Red Sox never finished higher than fifth in the AL. Just before the 1933 season, the team got a new owner, Tom Yawkey. His arrival started to turn things around.

Yawkey had money to spend. Because of that, the Red Sox picked up more star players. In 1935 Yawkey brought in Joe Cronin. The shortstop made five All-Star teams in Boston while also serving as the team's manager. First baseman Jimmie Foxx was one of the best power hitters of the day. He had already won two AL MVP Awards

Three-time AL MVP Jimmie Foxx led baseball in home runs four times during his career.

with the Philadelphia Athletics when he was traded to Boston in 1935. Two years later, he won the AL MVP.

However, perhaps the greatest Red Sox player ever showed up in 1939. Growing up in San Diego, Ted Williams had only one wish. "All I wanted out of life," said Williams, "is that when I walk down the street folks will say, 'There goes the greatest hitter that ever lived.'"

Williams was certainly one of baseball's best hitters right away. The left fielder hit .327 and led the AL with 145 RBIs in his rookie season. Tall and skinny, he earned the nickname "the Splendid Splinter."

Entering 1941 only 27 MLB players had ever hit over .400 in a season. It had not happened since 1930. Some wondered if anyone would ever do it again. Williams sat above the mark most of the year. But a small slump over the final three weeks dropped his average from .413 to .3995 entering the final day. The Red Sox were in Philadelphia for a doubleheader with the Athletics. If Williams didn't play, his average would round up to .400. Manager Joe Cronin offered to let Williams sit out. The left fielder refused.

Williams singled in his first at-bat in the top of the second inning. In the fifth, he hit a home run. Two more singles followed as the Red Sox rallied from 11–3 down to defeat the Athletics 12–11.

The slugger had two more hits in the second game. The 6-for-8 performance raised Williams's average to .406. Philadelphia fans mobbed him after the game. Williams's teammates had to help make sure no one stole his bat. Since Williams completed his feat, no other MLB player has hit .400 in a season.

## THE MAD DASH

It took five more years for Williams and the Red Sox to reach the World Series. In 1946 Boston faced off against the St. Louis Cardinals. Williams struggled in the series, batting only .200 and logging just one hit: an RBI. It was in part because St. Louis defended him with three infielders on the right side of second base. The "shift" is used often today. But in 1946 that tactic had rarely been seen. Williams, a left-handed hitter, had nowhere to pull the ball.

First baseman Rudy York and second basemen Bobby Doerr picked up the offensive slack for Boston. After six games, the series was tied. The seventh

## WILLIAMS AT WAR

Ted Williams might have had even better stats, but he missed three full seasons and parts of two more while serving in the military. After the United States entered World War II (1939–45), Williams was drafted and served as a pilot for the Navy. When the Korean War (1950–53) broke out, Williams was recalled. He flew 39 combat missions in that war.

game was in St. Louis. The Red Sox rallied for two runs in the top of the eighth inning to tie the game 3–3. But St. Louis right fielder Enos Slaughter led off the bottom half with a single. Three batters later, he scored from first base on left fielder Harry Walker's double. Boston shortstop Johnny Pesky hesitated on his relay throw to home, allowing Slaughter to slide in safely.

Boston never got another chance at the World Series in Williams's amazing career. He stayed with the Red Sox until 1960. In his final career at-bat, Williams clubbed a home run into the right-field seats at Fenway Park. That was a fitting end for a player who, in his 19 MLB seasons, hit under .300 only once.

Hall of Famer and two-time AL MVP Ted Williams played his entire 19-year MLB career with the Red Sox.

# CHAMPIONSHIP HEARTBREAK

One year after Ted Williams retired, another outfielder showed up in Boston to start a long, storied career with the Red Sox. Carl Yastrzemski first suited up for Boston on April 11, 1961. When he finally retired after 23 years with the Red Sox, "Yaz" had played in 3,308 games, the most in club history.

Yastrzemski won three AL batting titles in the 1960s. His best season came in 1967. Yastrzemski hit .326 with 44 home runs and 121 RBIs. All three totals led the AL, earning him the so-called "Triple Crown." It took 45 years until another MLB player won the Triple Crown, when Miguel Cabrera did it in 2012.

Hall of Famer Carl Yastrzemski watches his hit for the Red Sox. He played his entire 23-year career in Boston.

Pitcher Jim Lonborg joined the team in 1965 and two years later was named the Cy Young Award winner as the best pitcher in the league. Behind the team's excellent hitting and the pitching of Lonborg, manager Dick Williams's Red Sox stayed in contention all season. However, it was one of the tightest pennant races ever in the AL. Heading into the final weekend, four teams had a chance to win.

With two games remaining, Boston hosted Minnesota for the final two games of the season. Entering the series, the Twins were a game ahead of Boston in the standings. But in Game 1, Yastrzemski blasted a three-run home run in the seventh inning to help Boston build a 6–2 lead. The Red Sox's eventual 6–4 victory tied the teams for first place.

The next day, the Twins raced out to a 2–0 lead. Once again it was Yastrzemski who ignited the comeback. His RBI single in the bottom of the sixth started a five-run Red Sox rally that

## THE NIGHTMARE

The one downside to Boston's "Impossible Dream" season of 1967 was the horrible injury suffered by outfielder Tony Conigliaro. "Tony C." was a fan favorite who had grown up in the Boston area. He was only 22 years old in 1967. But he had already hit 104 home runs when he was hit in the eye by a pitch on August 18. The injury was so severe he didn't play again until 1969. Due to permanent eye damage, his career lasted only 382 more games.

Red Sox pitcher and Cy Young Award winner Jim Lonborg led the league in strikeouts (246) and all of baseball in wins (22) during the 1967 season.

claimed the pennant. Boston fans called the 1967 season "the Impossible Dream."

The World Series featured another matchup with the St. Louis Cardinals. Yastrzemski was brilliant again. He hit .400 with three home runs in the seven-game series. That helped the Red Sox erase a 3–1 series deficit. But Boston had no answer for St. Louis ace Bob Gibson in Game 7. The right-hander struck out 10 Red Sox hitters in a complete game 7–2 win. Gibson added insult to injury by hitting a home run in the fifth inning. Just as they had in 1946, the Red Sox came up just short. It had been 49 years since the team last won a title.

## STAY FAIR

The Impossible Dream season started a run of 16 straight winning records for the Red Sox. But even though MLB expanded the playoffs in 1969, Boston did not reach the World Series again until 1975. That year's AL champions were loaded. Yastrzemski, now playing first base, was still solid at 35 years old. Left fielder Jim Rice led the team with 22 home runs though an injury caused him to sit out that year's World Series. Center fielder Fred Lynn was both AL MVP and Rookie of the Year. No player had ever done that before. Pitchers Luis Tiant and Bill "Spaceman" Lee anchored the staff.

Jim Rice, the 1978 AL MVP, led the league in hits (213), triples (15), home runs (46), and RBIs (139) that season.

However, the team's rock was sixth-year catcher Carlton Fisk. The New Hampshire native was an excellent defender and hit .331 during the season. The Red Sox rolled to a 95–65 record and swept the Oakland Athletics in the AL Championship Series (ALCS). That set up what turned out to be a classic World Series against the Cincinnati Reds.

The Red Sox won the first game 6–0 behind Tiant's strong pitching. But the Reds, nicknamed "the Big Red Machine" for their powerful lineup, won three of the next four. The teams headed back to Boston for Game 6 but had to wait three extra days to play due to the rainy fall weather in Boston. When they finally got on the field, the Reds and Red Sox delivered an epic clash.

Boston raced out to a 3–0 lead in the bottom of the first inning. The Reds then scored six unanswered runs. Still down 6–3 with two outs in the bottom of the eighth inning, pinch hitter Bernie Carbo tied it up with a dramatic three-run homer to center field.

After several close calls, the game was still tied in the bottom of the 12th. Fisk led off for Boston. Cincinnati reliever Pat Darcy's second pitch was a low fastball. Fisk, who was a right-handed hitter, went down to a knee and golfed the ball down the left-field line. The crowd knew Fisk had hit it far enough. But everyone was wondering if it would stay

Red Sox catcher Carlton Fisk, *left*, watches his hit sail out of the stadium in the 12th inning of Game 6 of the 1975 World Series.

fair. Fisk never took his eye off the ball as he waved his arms to the right, as if guiding the ball. It eventually struck the foul pole for a home run. As the crowd erupted and Fisk circled the bases, the organist at Fenway Park played the "Hallelujah Chorus."

Even though Boston lost Game 7 the next day, Fisk's home run remains one of the most famous World Series moments.

Fisk would later say of the series that Boston "won that series three games to four."

## THE MELTDOWN

Boston had to wait another 11 years to reach the World Series again. Rice was still with the Red Sox in 1986, as was right fielder Dwight Evans. Now Boston's lineup also featured smooth-swinging third baseman Wade Boggs. The team also had a hard-throwing right-handed pitcher from Texas named Roger Clemens. In April of that year, Clemens set an MLB record by striking out 20 batters in a single game. He finished the year 24–4 and walked away with the first of his record seven Cy Young Awards.

A dramatic comeback in the ALCS against the

Hall of Fame third baseman Wade Boggs played 11 of his 18 major league seasons with the Red Sox.

First baseman Bill Buckner walks off the field after committing an error that caused the New York Mets' winning run to cross home plate in Game 7 of the 1986 World Series.

California Angels pitted Boston against the New York Mets for the championship. Once again the series turned on a dramatic Game 6. Boston held a 3–2 series lead for the game in New York's Shea Stadium. Red Sox outfielder Dave Henderson broke a 3–3 tie with a two-run home run in the top of the 10th inning. And after Boston reliever Calvin Schiraldi got the first two outs in the bottom half, it appeared that the curse was about to end.

The Mets' stadium scoreboard even briefly flashed a message that read: "Congratulations Red Sox."

Then it all fell apart. Schiraldi allowed three consecutive singles as the Mets got one run back. Right-hander Bob Stanley then took over on the mound for Boston with runners on first and third. Facing New York outfielder Mookie Wilson, Stanley's 2–2 pitch missed catcher Rich Gedman and went to the backstop. Kevin Mitchell scored for the Mets, with Ray Knight moving over to second base.

Just when Boston fans thought it couldn't get any worse, Wilson hit a bouncing ball to first base. Playing there for the Red Sox was 36-year-old Bill Buckner. Boston manager John McNamara usually brought a defensive substitute in for Buckner late in games, as the veteran had bad knees. But in Game 6, McNamara left Buckner in. The mistake cost the Red Sox the game, as Wilson's grounder bounced through Buckner's legs into right field. Knight raced home to give the Mets an incredible 6–5 win.

The Red Sox still had a chance in Game 7. But the shattered team blew a 3–0 lead in the late innings and lost 8–5. As the Mets celebrated a championship, Boston fans wept. The Curse of the Bambino seemed only to be getting stronger. Despite several appearances, the Red Sox didn't win another playoff series until 1998.

MILLAR
15
BOSTON
RAMIREZ
24

# A DYNASTY RENEWED

**W**hat made the Red Sox's failures even worse was the success of their biggest rival, the New York Yankees. Before Babe Ruth went to New York, the team had never won a title. But after the 2000 season, the championship count stood at Yankees 26, Red Sox 5.

Things had always been heated between the two clubs on the field. However, in the early 2000s the rivalry went up several degrees. Both Boston and New York spent big money assembling superteams.

In 2003 Boston thought it had caught up to New York. The Red Sox had a fierce lineup led by shortstop Nomar Garciaparra, outfielder Manny Ramirez, catcher Jason Varitek,

Designated hitter David Ortiz celebrates after hitting a two-run homer against the New York Yankees in Game 1 of the 2003 ALCS.

and designated hitter David "Big Papi" Ortiz. On the mound, righty Pedro Martínez baffled hitters with multiple highly skilled pitches.

The two teams met in the ALCS. After six close games, Game 7 was held at Yankee Stadium. Ortiz hit a home run in the top of the eighth to put Boston up 5–2. That lead looked safe with Martínez cruising on the mound. However, he was tired. Boston manager Grady Little still refused to take Martínez out, and New York scored three times in the bottom of the eight to tie it up. The Red Sox's pain increased in the bottom of the 11th when Yankees third baseman Aaron Boone hit a walk-off home run.

## THE COMEBACK

Boston bounced right back in 2004. The team had a new manager in Terry Francona. Right-handed pitcher Curt Schilling was brought in to strengthen the pitching staff. Ramirez and Ortiz both hit more than 40 home runs. Catcher Varitek added strength behind the plate. First baseman Kevin Millar and centerfielder Johnny Damon rounded out the lineup.

The Red Sox also had a carefree attitude. By now the pressure on Red Sox teams to end the 86-year drought was huge. But Boston's players seemed to laugh it off. Millar was asked how the players handled it. "We have a bunch

Three-time Cy Young Award winner Pedro Martínez pitches against the New York Yankees in Game 7 of the 2003 ALCS.

of idiots," he said. "We go out there, we're ugly and we just have fun."

No Red Sox fan was having fun after the Yankees raced out to a 3–0 lead in the 2004 ALCS. Game 3 was especially bad, as New York blew out Boston 19–8 at Fenway Park.

No MLB team had ever come back from 3–0 down to win a playoff series. But Millar's confidence still wasn't rattled.

As cameras followed him around before Game 4, he told everyone, "Just don't let us win tonight!" Millar felt that if the team could win Game 4, their talent would carry them on to win the series.

Ortiz backed up Millar's talk. Boston tied the game with no outs in the ninth inning. Then Big Papi won it on a two-run homer in the 12th. Ortiz walked off Game 5 as well with an RBI single in the 14th inning. It was a 3–2 series headed back to New York.

After Boston won Game 6, everything changed. Boston fans who wrote off the team after Game 3 showed up at Yankee Stadium to witness history. They saw Ortiz hit a two-run homer in the first inning. Then Damon hit two home runs, including a grand slam in the second. The Red Sox routed New York 10–3.

The World Series once again featured a matchup with the St. Louis Cardinals, who had beaten Boston in 1946 and 1967. Both of those series were decided in seven games. This Red Sox team was determined not to let it get that far. Boston never trailed

## THE BLOODY SOCK GAME

Curt Schilling was scheduled to pitch Game 6 of the 2004 ALCS. Earlier in the playoffs, he had torn a tendon in his ankle. But a team doctor surgically repaired it enough so that the righty could try to play. Despite bleeding through his sock, Schilling shut down the Yankees for seven innings as Boston won 4–1.

Red Sox ace Curt Schilling led the majors in wins (21) during Boston's 2004 World Series championship season.

once in a dominant four-game sweep. When closer Keith Foulke fielded a grounder to record the final out of Game 4, all of New England celebrated. The Red Sox had been three outs away from being eliminated in Game 4 of the ALCS. They then won eight consecutive games to finally break the 86-year streak without a championship.

"If we were going to do it after 86 years," said team general manager Theo Epstein, "we figured we might as well do it in style."

## BIG PAPI

Boston's next title wait was not nearly as long. Three years later, the Red Sox were back. They cruised in the World Series again. Boston outscored the upstart Colorado Rockies 29–10 in another four-game sweep.

Several stars from the 2004 team had already moved on. Those that remained were getting older. Schilling was 40 in 2007. Varitek and Ramirez were both 35. Boston came within a game of going back to the World Series in 2008, but by 2012 the aging team was struggling. Francona had left as manager, and Boston finished last at 69–93.

Ortiz was the only Red Sox player still left from 2004. He was on the tail end of an amazing career. Ortiz had come to Boston in 2003 after the Minnesota Twins let him go. He never expected to be a superstar, but his big hits and fun-loving personality quickly made him the heart of the Red Sox. When Ortiz finally retired, he had played more games than all but

The 2004 Boston Red Sox celebrate their World Series win over the St. Louis Cardinals.

Ortiz rips a single in Game 5 of the 2013 World Series against the St. Louis Cardinals.

four Boston players. And only Ted Williams had hit more home runs in a Red Sox uniform.

Before Ortiz left, however, he still helped Boston to one of the great turnarounds in MLB history. With Ortiz slugging a team-high 30 homers, the 2013 Red Sox bounced back and won the AL East Division.

Once again Boston found itself in the World Series against the Cardinals. This time it took the Red Sox six games to claim another title. The 37-year-old Ortiz won series MVP after hitting an amazing .688 with two home runs. However, the biggest story after clinching Game 6 of the series was where it happened. When the Red Sox won in 2004, the clinching game came in St. Louis. The 2007 series ended in Denver. Game 6 in 2013 took place at Fenway Park. The Red Sox clinched a World Series win at home for the first time since 1918.

## FULL CIRCLE

Ortiz retired after the 2016 season. Two years later, a new crop of players were leading the way for the Red Sox. Boston won a team-record 108 games under first-year manager Alex Cora. Right fielder Mookie Betts captured the AL batting title and MVP Award. Shortstop Xander Bogaerts was also among the AL's best players. And the Red Sox once again had a dominant pitching staff led by left-handers Chris Sale and David Price.

## BOSTON STRONG

The Red Sox dedicated their 2013 championship to the victims of the bombing of the Boston Marathon the previous April. After the series was over, David Ortiz spoke to the crowd and said, "This is for you, Boston. You guys deserve it. We've been through a lot this year, and this is for all of you and all those families who struggled."

After years of the Red Sox being "cursed," *from left*, Steve Pearce, David Ortiz, Mike Lowell, and Manny Ramirez show off the team's four World Series trophies won from 2004 to 2018.

As a result of these talented players' efforts, Boston made it to the World Series n 2018. However, the team's World Series hero seemingly came out of nowhere. Steve Pearce was 35 years old in 2018. He had already played for six other MLB teams when he joined Boston as a backup halfway through the season. He started in the playoffs only after first baseman Mitch Moreland was hurt.

After a quiet first few games against the Los Angeles Dodgers, Pearce's bat woke up in Game 4. The veteran hit a game-tying home run in the top of the eighth inning at Dodger Stadium. The homer helped Boston rally from 4–0 down to win 9–6.

The Red Sox were up 3–1 in the series. Incredibly, Pearce hit two more home runs in Game 5. His second put Boston up 5–1 in the eighth inning. After Boston held that lead, Pearce was named series MVP.

Boston's fourth World Series win of the 2000s came with controversy. It was determined that the Red Sox had used a video monitor in the clubhouse to steal signs from other teams during the year. In addition Cora was suspended for the 2020 season due to his involvement in a different sign-stealing scandal with the Houston Astros.

Four-time Silver Slugger Xander Bogaerts made his MLB debut with the Red Sox in 2013.

A century after Harry Frazee got rid of Babe Ruth and sank a Red Sox dynasty, the team's fans hoped another mistake wouldn't do the same. After his suspension and a grace period after his firing, Cora returned in 2021 and eased fans' fears. He led Boston back to the ALCS.

# TIMELINE

**1901**

The Boston Americans join seven other teams to create the American League.

**1903**

Boston defeats the Pittsburgh Pirates 5–3 in the first World Series.

**1907**

Boston owner John Taylor officially gives the team its nickname of "Red Sox" to be used starting in the 1908 season.

**1912**

Fenway Park opens, and the Red Sox defeat the New York Giants in the World Series.

**1918**

Boston defeats the Chicago Cubs 4–2 to win its third World Series in four years.

**1919**

Boston owner Harry Frazee sells Ruth's contract to the rival New York Yankees for $100,000.

**1933**

Tom Yawkey purchases the Red Sox, beginning 70 years of ownership by his family.

**1941**

Williams goes 6-for-8 in a doubleheader on the final day of the season to raise his batting average to .406. He is the first AL or NL player in 11 years to finish over .400 for a season.

**1946**

The Red Sox reach the World Series for the first time since 1918 but lose in seven games to the NL-champion St. Louis Cardinals.

## 1967

Led by Triple Crown winner Carl Yastrzemski, the "Impossible Dream" Red Sox win the AL pennant on the season's final day. However, Boston loses a seven-game World Series to the Cardinals.

## 1975

Despite catcher Carlton Fisk's dramatic game-winning home run in Game 6, the Red Sox lose another seven-game World Series, this time to the Cincinnati Reds.

## 1986

Despite leading 5–3 with two outs in the bottom of the 10th inning of Game 6, Boston collapses and loses the World Series to the New York Mets in seven games.

## 2004

After rallying from 3–0 down in the ALCS against the Yankees, Boston sweeps St. Louis in the World Series for its first championship in 86 years.

## 2007

The Red Sox win the World Series again, sweeping the Colorado Rockies.

## 2013

Boston beats the Cardinals 4–2 to win its third championship in 10 years. The Red Sox clinch the title at Fenway Park for the first time since 1918.

## 2018

Boston defeats the Los Angeles Dodgers 4–1 to become the first team to reach four World Series titles in the 2000s.

# TEAM FACTS

## FRANCHISE HISTORY

Boston Americans (1901–07)
Boston Red Sox (1907– )

## WORLD SERIES CHAMPIONSHIPS

1903, 1912, 1915, 1916, 1918,
2004, 2007, 2013, 2018

## KEY PLAYERS

Mookie Betts (2014–19)
Xander Bogaerts (2013– )
Wade Boggs (1982–92)
Roger Clemens (1984–96)
Bobby Doerr (1937–44,
   1946–51)
Carlton Fisk (1969–80)
Harry Hooper (1909–20)
Pedro Martínez (1998–04)
David Ortiz (2003–16)
Dustin Pedroia (2006–19)
Manny Ramirez (2001–08)
Jim Rice (1974–89)
Babe Ruth (1914–19)
Tris Speaker (1907–15)
Luis Tiant (1971–78) (9)

Ted Williams (1939–42,
   1946–60)
Smoky Joe Wood (1908–15)
Carl Yastrzemski (1961–83)
Cy Young (1901–08)

## KEY MANAGERS

Jimmy Collins (1901–06)
Alex Cora (2018–19, 2021– )
Joe Cronin (1935–47)
Terry Francona (2004–11)

## HOME STADIUMS

Huntington Avenue Grounds
   (1901–11)
Fenway Park (1912– )

## POLE TO POLE

Both foul poles at Fenway Park have official names. The left-field pole is the "Fisk Pole" after catcher Carlton Fisk's home run in the 1975 World Series. The right-field pole is "Pesky's Pole" after former Red Sox infielder Johnny Pesky. Pesky's Pole is also covered in thousands of signatures from players and fans.

## AWARD WINNER

In addition to winning the 2018 AL batting title and MVP Award, Red Sox outfielder Mookie Betts also won the Silver Slugger and Gold Glove Awards. When he won the World Series as well, Betts became the first player in MLB history to win all four awards and a championship in the same season.

## SELLING OUT

From May 15, 2003, to April 10, 2013, the Red Sox did not have a single unsold ticket at Fenway Park. The 794-game regular-season streak is the longest in American professional sports. Including playoff games, Boston sold out 820 games in a row.

## SWEET CAROLINE

One of the Red Sox's newest traditions, beginning in the late 1990s, is the singing of the Neil Diamond song "Sweet Caroline" during the eighth inning of each home game. When Diamond was given the Kennedy Center Honors in 2011, singer Smokey Robinson sang the song on stage backed by 80 Red Sox fans.

# GLOSSARY

**ace**

A team's best starting pitcher.

**backstop**

The high fence directly behind home plate on a baseball or softball field.

**designated hitter**

A player who bats in place of a teammate.

**dynasty**

A team that has an extended period of success, usually winning multiple championships in the process.

**general manager**

An executive who runs a team and is responsible for finding and signing players.

**iconic**

Well known for excellence.

**pennant**

Another name for a league championship; in MLB, refers to winning either the American or National League.

**pull**

When the hitter drives the ball to the side of the field on which they are standing.

**rival**

An opponent with whom a player or team has a fierce and ongoing competition.

**upstart**

A newly successful team that is not expected to win.

**walk-off**

Any victory in which the home team scores the winning run in the bottom of the final inning.

# MORE INFORMATION

## BOOKS

Flynn, Brendan. *The MLB Encyclopedia*. Minneapolis, MN: Abdo Publishing, 2022.

Hewson, Anthony K. *GOATs of Baseball*. Minneapolis, MN: Abdo Publishing, 2022.

Mitchell, Bo. *Ultimate MLB Road Trip*. Minneapolis, MN: Abdo Publishing, 2019.

## ONLINE RESOURCES

To learn more about the Boston Red Sox, please visit **abdobooklinks.com** or scan this QR code. These links are routinely monitored and updated to provide the most current information available.

# INDEX



## ABOUT THE AUTHOR

David J. Clarke is a freelance writer. Originally from Helena, Montana, he now lives in Savannah, Georgia, with his golden retriever, Gus.